A Funny Thing Happened at the Doctor's Office

A Funny Thing Happened at the Doctor's Office

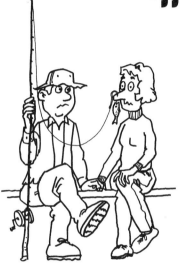

Thomas G. Briggs, MD

Beaver's Pond Press

ISBN 0-890676-07-1

J I H G F E D C B A

Printed in the United States of America

Production Editor: Milton E. Adams
Interior Design: Mori Studio
Cover Design and Cartoons: Tom Blessing

Beaver's Pond Press

5125 Danen's Drive
Edina, Minnesota 55439-1465
612-829-8818
Fax: 612-944-4065
E-mail: adamsppo@aol.com

Dedicated to:

Joan, Gary, Steve, Laura...
and my patients.

Thanks

I wish to acknowledge my associate Doctor's:
Miles Lane, Carol Stark, Terry Henderson, Curt Keller,
Al Fetzek, Jeanne Anderson, Tom Nichols, Hector Brown,
Milt Ingermann, Carrol Ramsayer, Charles Beck, Bob Flom,
Ted Watson, Charles McCarthy, and others.

To Connie Anderson for her editorial assistance.

To Milt Adams, my publisher.

To Tom Blessing, dear friend and artist
who illustrated this book so well.

To my friends for their help and encouragement.

A Funny Thing Happened at the Doctor's Office

Foreword

The doctor's office can often be a serious place. However, some funny things do happen there, and at the hospital. After 40 years of medical school, internship, military flight surgeon, and then family practice, I've added my stories to those of my colleagues.

The hospital social worker was talking to an unwed woman who had just given birth. They were talking about placing the baby for adoption, and information needed for the birth certificate.

The social worker wanted more information about the father. What was his height, weight, and nationality. The mother didn't have any accurate answers for these questions.

Finally the social worker asked, "What color hair did he have?" The woman said, "I don't know, he didn't take his hat off."

Frequently during deliveries, doctors refer to the head of the baby when it enters the largest part of the pelvis "to be engaged," that is, it is through the largest part. Medical jargon shouldn't alarm patients. However, one woman, upon hearing the doctor say, "she's engaged," the woman corrected the doctor. "I am married, not just engaged."

• • •

While interning, I had a little problem with my scrub suit. The suit had numerous ties and one time, after delivering a baby, I pulled the wrong string, and my scrub pants dropped to the floor, to the amazement of most of the personnel, and to my embarrassment.

• • •

Medical school students have a very weird sense of humor. One of my classmates examined a female patient. When he was done, he picked up a broom, took off his white coat, and said, "The doctor will be in in a moment, ma'm."

Overheard in a clinic waiting room years ago: A young boy was visiting with a nun who was dressed in the traditional habit. The young boy asked, "What are you wearing?" The nun replied, "This is my habit."

The boy said, "Yes, I know, my sister has a lot of bad habits, too," and at that he turned back to his mother and informed her he had been talking to "this nut here."

• • •

When the nurse alerted me there was a frantic mother on the phone, I was prepared for almost anything. The mother said, "My little girl has put an eye in her vagina!"

As I waited for them at the clinic, I wondered how she had somehow inserted an artificial eye. Upon examining the little girl, I discovered it was truly an "I," a plastic magnetized "I" that children play with.

A rather well-endowed young woman came into my clinic with a terrible chest cold. Usually I would ask a patient to open her mouth and take a big breath. Unfortunately, this time I said, "Now open your mouth and take a big breast in."

The county hospital emergency room had a frequent guest who would get drunk, get thrown in jail,and then claim he was vomiting blood in order to get out of jail. When he was brought to the hospital, we admitted him because we found blood in his vomit.

On one occasion, a smart colleague looked at the blood under a microscope and discovered animal blood. We discovered that to get out of jail, the drunk would swallow capsules of chicken blood.

• • •

Years ago, a rather anxious patient of mine was constantly concerned about his heart. He owned the local variety store in town. One day he was downstairs in his store. At that time, the store used a chute for deliveries to be sent down from the street level. The last package received that day was the delivery man himself who had died of a heart attack and fell forward and came down the chute to the basement. My patient made an emergency visit to see me at the clinic to have *his* heart checked.

Doctors of all kinds love to play jokes on other doctors. It's not too often patients play jokes on them.

A young woman was a roommate of another young lady dental student. On the first visit, the dentist told her she would need a procedure to correct her jutting lower jaw.

After discussing this with her roommate, the dental student rehearsed her as to what to say on her return visit.

At the next visit, the dentist said to her, "Now we'll have to put braces on, and I want to explain what else is needed."

That's when the patient replied, "Yes, I know. I have an imperfect bite, and the medial buccal cuspid of #19 is not occluding with the buccal groove of #14. This scares me because there is a humongous chance of having class 3 surgery.

The dentist stared in disbelief and said, "What kind of work do you do?"

She replied, "I'm a hair dresser". The astonished dentist was then let in on the little joke.

A male doctor was examining a new infant with both the mother and father watching him. As the father was diapering the child after the exam, the mother asked the doctor about vitamins and formula. Then she asked, "How about sexual relations?"

The doctor responded, "I would like to, but I'm married you know." The father, busy with the infant said, "I don't think she meant you!"

• • •

A black mother called into the clinic and informed me her daughter had anemia. I asked, "What kind?"

The distraught mother replied, "The sick-as-hell anemia." (Black people can develop a special kind of anemia called sickle cell anemia because the blood cell is shaped like a sickle.)

Doctors are creatures of habit. One doctor, when visiting another city for a medical convention, was checking for the fire escapes in his hotel.

He opened a door and there was a man sitting on the toilet. The doctor excused himself and said, "I was looking for the fire escapes," and closed the door.

A split second later, the man was out the door with his pants around his ankles, shouting, "Where's the fire?"

Meconium is a stool substance from a fetus. In the delivery room, one of the doctors stated, "Here comes meconium." This is what the mother ended up naming the child.

• • •

The doctor said to the patient, "Please undress to the waist." When he turned around expecting to examine her chest area, the women had taken off everything from the waist down.

• • •

A patient inquired of the doctor about having vasectomy, but wondered if it could be reversed. The doctor asked, "Why?" The patient replied, "Well, in case my wife dies." The doctor said, "That won't bring her back."

• • •

The patient asked the doctor for a prescription for a cold. The doctor took the prescription pad and wrote, "One cold."

A well-known doctor was invited to Russia to give a lecture. He had heard that the hotels often have listening devices in the rooms, so he proceeded to check. He looked behind the mirrors and under the mattress. He even rolled up the rug, and there he found it. A hexagonal metal object which he proceeded to unscrew. Seconds later, the chandelier crashed to floor in the room below.

This same consultant was asked to study why workers at the Kennedy Space Center had a heart attack rate two and a half times the national average. He thinks he found out. He described the personnel director as having "all the warmth and compassion of a social worker at Auschwitz."

● ● ●

An area treatment center for alcoholic women is called Dia Linn, which in Gaelic means "In God We Trust."
Our clinic doctors worked with the women in treatment there, and one of my colleagues was at Dia Linn when a specialist called for him. Our clinic receptionist said, "That doctor is at Dia Linn." The specialist dialed the number but visualized the other doctor spending his Wednesday afternoon at a card-playing place. A woman's voice answered, "Dia Linn, Virginia speaking." He thought this might be the madame. He then asked, "Is Doctor Smith there." She replied, "Yes, but he's upstairs with one of the ladies."

Then the specialist was *sure* he was correct.

It was almost nine o'clock in the evening and my partner was tired from working late. He was closing up his clinic door to leave. A young man screeched around the corner in his VW Beetle and came to a halt in front of the office door. He indicated he was happy to see a doctor still there. The doctor mumbled something about he wasn't so sure he was happy to be there yet.

The doctor asked what was wrong. The young man said he'd been in an accident a few days back, and now that he had seen his lawyer, he was supposed to come in and get a bunch of x-rays.

The doctor asked if he hurt any place, and the man said, "No, my lawyer said to come get a bunch of x-rays."

The doctor proceeded to open the door and went into the clinic. A few minutes later he returned with a cardboard box full of discarded x-rays. He told the young man to hold out his hands. "What's this?" he asked. The doctor said, "A bunch of x-rays!"

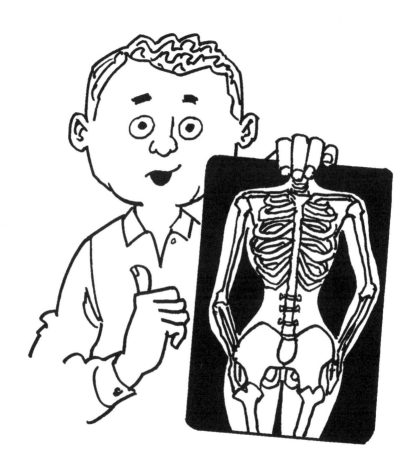

There's the concept that some alcoholics need to "hit bottom" to realize they need help.

A patient recounted that he had been in Alaska in his float plane, hunting polar bears. He got intoxicated and wandered off. Eskimos rescued him afloat on a ice flow.

His "hit bottom" was cold, and moving out to sea.

• • •

One of my partners was working late in his office. The phone rang and a mother asked, "What was wrong with my teenager when you saw him today?"

The doctor then realized he had never seen the 16-year-old. He rushed to an examining room and found the boy asleep on the x-ray table. He wakened the boy and said, "Okay, we are ready to take the x-rays now," treated him and sent him home.

An elderly patient was being seen by one of our surgical colleagues. The doctor was examining the man and had him upside down on a specially-designed Ritter table used for doing a proctoscopy (a hollow rectal tube). The surgeon noticed a lesion that was snipped out and proceeded to use an electric needle to coagulate the bleeding spot.

This electric needle set off a loud explosion of rectal methane gas with a real "KABOOM!" The explosion blew the surgeon back across the room on his roller stool, and caused the patient to cry out, "J---- C-----, what was that?"

• • •

The hospital switchboard operator answered the phone. The woman said she was calling to schedule an autopsy. The operator told her she had to die first!

A 17-year old unwed young woman was visiting the doctor. She was a diabetic and seven months pregnant. Usually babies of diabetics are larger than normal. The doctor noticed this baby was rather small.

"How big was the father?" the doctor asked to gain some insights.

"Oh, about this big," she said, as she held up her index fingers 12 inches apart.

A surgical resident was in his first year of residency at the University of Minnesota. However, because he had an infection (paronychia) around his fingernail, he was prohibited from scrubbing up and participating in the operation. When the stern professor came in, he asked where Dr. Brown was. The others indicated he was in the observation dome above the teaching operating area.

Brown happened to have the infection on the end of his middle finger. To reinforce what the others had told the professor, he held up that finger, pointing it at the surgeon.

This movement (not well thought out), caused other residents around him great glee.

• • •

A rather attractive woman was a patient at our clinic. My partner, who is a real joker, commented to his nurse after the patient left, "I want to go to bed with her again." The nurse questioned, "What do you mean AGAIN?!! The doctor said, "Well, I had wanted to once before."

A pregnant woman was in an ambulance that was escorted by the police. She alerted the ambulance personnel that delivery was eminent. They pulled into a motel and the father-to-be asked the clerk to give them a key to an empty room.

When they arrived at the room, it wasn't empty and the chain latch was on. The expectant father and a police officer put their shoulders to the door. To everyone's surprise, there was a young couple, au naturale, having intercourse. The male fled to the bathroom and the female wrapped herself in the sheet while they proceeded to bring the pregnant woman. The baby was born, with the young woman still wrapped in the sheet next to the new mother.

The new father went to the front desk to protest why he was given an occupied room. The clerk said it was supposed to be empty. Evidently, this couple had been using it for their get togethers for some time. Odds are they won't do that again.

• • •

A colleague said, "I never met a psychiatrist that didn't need one."

As I often do, I said "I suppose a tiger bit you" to a young lady who came in with a scratch.

"No, a leopard scratched me." She had gotten too close to the leopard cage and the leopard scratched her.

A bunch of Minnesota guys regularly went skiing together. One of the men tended to drink too much. I gave him pills and told him they might help him with his hangovers and adjustment to the altitude. He couldn't wait to get them down.

What he was given was a methylene blue pill that is used to record urine dye when it goes down a wrong track. Of course, to track it properly, it turns the urine blue.

The next morning as we were at the top of the Aspen Mountain, this hard drinker was relieving himself in the trough. Standing between two startled strangers, his urine came out blue. Usually not one to be at a loss of words, this time he was. His revenge was to threaten to write my name in blue in the snow at the next rest stop.

The man's wife said he should tell everyone he's from Minnesota - the "Land of Sky Blue Water."

• • •

A patient of mine called to ask if birth control pills worked at 10 in the morning. I wanted to say, "No, it shuts down between 8 and noon," but I reassured her they were effective at 10 a.m.

One of my partner's nurses worked for him a number of years. They respected each other greatly but enjoyed sparring with each other. One day she called my partner at the hospital and after the conversation had gone on for some time, she said, "You know, Dr. Smith, you are going to give me an inferiority complex." He replied, "It's no complex."

• • •

One of the clinic's long-time clients died at the hospital following surgery, and two doctors attended the funeral. The doctor overheard people speaking of the deceased. "She really looks good," one said.

"She should," the other said, "she just got out of the hospital."

• • •

In an exam, a doctor was surprised to find that a young woman had tattooed under one breast, "Sweet," and under the other, "Sour."

One of my patients owned a car dealership called "Country Dealership." As part of this country motif, he had a little farm with farm animals such as sheep, pigs, chickens, turkeys, etc. One day I was visiting the dealership and had been looking at the farm animals over the fence. A little piglet was flanked out with its legs fore and aft. A little lamb came up and butted it right in the side. This caused the piglet to scamper off. The lamb followed with its unique "pogo stick" bouncy running style.

I turned to a mother and her three children and said, "You ought to see this," and when I turned back, the lamb had mounted the pig.

As I suspected, she never saw me again as a patient.

While stationed as a flight surgeon in the Washington, D.C. area, there was a flight surgeon colonel we figured must have gotten his medical degree out of a punch board. We hoped the Russians had a counterpart.

Before the use of image-intensifier x-ray machines, it was necessary to use rose-colored glasses to allow the eyes to dilate to see images better on a fluoroscope for 20 minutes.

This colonel felt since there may be light leaks in his goggles, he stuffed rags inside. Now he couldn't see at all. So he had his airman help him dress in the morning in his dress bird colonel uniform, escort him to his car, drive him to the Pentagon, escort him through the door to the elevator. He was wearing his rose-colored glasses with the rags hanging out when he arrived at his office to do a fluoroscopy.

• • •

A patient of mine had a three-legged dog. The man said, "Come mating season, that dog doesn't even know he's handicapped."

One of my partners was attending a medical conference in Florida. When the delayed professor finally arrived, he explained that when he came up to an open draw bridge, he was behind a car that had a bumper sticker that said, "If you love Jesus, honk." Because he had nothing else to do while waiting, and because he loved Jesus as much as the next person, he honked. With this, the young man in the car rolled down the window and gave the doctor the bird.

• • •

It took the new doctor a extraordinarily long time to feel for lesions in the abdomen during a pelvic exam on a rather obese patient. Finally the patient said to him, "Doctor, you keep fooling around down there and you're going to ring my bell."

• • •

A patient came into my office and said he had been to the Veteran's Hospital. They told him he had the worst case of shingles they'd every seen. I was very interested and anxious to see his severe case of shingles. This patient, a real joker, had put one regular roofing shingle on his chest.

A woman patient requested care, but insisted there be no drugs. The doctor raised his hands and spread them out and declared, "HEAL."

A patient of mine waited unusually long to get married. In fact, she got married in the labor room of our hospital. A Justice of the Peace was requested, and between pains, she and her fiancee got married. Just prior to the baby being born, they were declared man and wife.

• • •

When I was a flight surgeon in Washington, D.C., my associate in the next office cried out plaintively, "Tom, Tom, help!" The doctor had been doing a rectal exam on a very heavy-set Colonel when the man fainted. I had to lift the passed-out patient off my associate's finger and body.

• • •

A man called the hospital and asked to have the new Hungarian-born doctor paged. The receptionist did page Dr. Yourowndink two times – and then realized she had been the brunt of a joke.

A friend of mine was really quite heavy. He kept kidding me, "Tom, that diet you put me on. Is it really supposed to be 15,000 calories. Shouldn't it be 1,500? I have to get up in the middle of the night to eat, I have to stop on the way to work, I can't get anything done, I am eating all the time."

The doctor entered the room, ready to examine a man lying on his stomach, covered by a sheet.

When the doctor lifted the sheet in preparation of doing a procto exam, the patient had a tape across his bottom that said, "I'd rather be golfing."

• • •

One of my more earthy patients called and left a message with the nurse that she had a boil on her butt. When I returned the call I said, "Hi, Gail, this is Dr. Briggs. I understand you have a boil on your butt."

There was a pause followed by "Who is this?"

Then I asked, "Isn't this 455-3355?"

After the person on the other end said, "No," I apologized and then hung up.

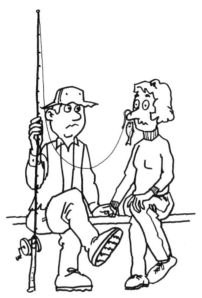

An anxious newlywed couple was waiting for the doctor in Exam Room 3. The husband had cast his fishing rod and unfortunately snagged his new wife in the nose. In their excitement, they never thought to cut the line, but instead reeled the wife closer in and went to shore. Now in the office, the husband was holding a fishing rod with the line running to the hook and minnow caught in his wife's nose. The doctor looked right at her and deadpanned, "And now what seems to be the problem?"

Years ago, a young doctor new in practice did a no-no, he pre-signed prescriptions, which were stolen. A pharmacist became suspicious when the thief came into the pharmacy with a prescription made out for "mo-pheen, 1 lb."

• • •

A woman doctor was telling colleagues that she overheard her son talking to friends. Most of her friends were also women doctors. The little boy said, "You know, boys can be doctors, too."

• • •

The young woman in delivery was pushing and straining. Her husband said, "I heard that the head is the hardest part – is that true? Without missing a beat, the nurse said, "I think the next 18 years are."

An elderly man entered the doctor's office with a rather unsteady painful-looking gait. When the doctor looked down, he noticed that the patient had his shoes on the wrong feet. He helped the man change his shoes to the right feet. The happy patient announced to all in the waiting room that the "doctor sure had magic hands."

A 80-year-old man was suffering from quite severe senility. But he hadn't loss his sex drive. The elderly wife asked her children to do something. She told them he'd demand sex four to five times a day . . . but two hours after intercourse, he'd demand it again because he forgot he just had sex. And if she'd refused, he'd sit in the car and pout.

Doing a family history, the nurse practitioner discovered that the patient had listed nine step sisters and five step brothers. NONE shared the same father or mother.

• • •

A young mother brought her 8-year-old son back to have his ears rechecked. While she was waiting for the doctor, she picked up what she thought was a large model of an ear. She was showing her son where the sound went and realized to her embarrassment she was sticking her finger through the pelvic model's vaginal opening. (The models do look a bit alike if the pelvic model is turned sidewise like an ear.)

She told the doctor later she would spread her legs to hear better.

• • •

Two salesmen were talking. They tended to travel together. Bob said, "Sam, I'm Catholic, and if I am ever injured or sick, be sure to call a priest."

Sam said, "Bob, I'm Jewish, and if I'm ever sick or injured, please call a doctor."

A new mother was approached by the hospital social worker, asking who the father was. She said she didn't know. The social worker said, "You don't know who the father is?"

The new mother replied, "If you sat on a pincushion, would you know which pin was pricking you?"

Years ago, in the days of house calls by doctors, a doctor received elaborate directions to a home by the patient. He followed her directions, but never found the home. He returned to his office as she called asking where he was. He explained he followed the directions. Then the woman thought about it and said, "Oh, I was standing the wrong way. I gave you the directions backwards."

• • •

One day I saw a 6'4" woman come down the hall of our clinic, dressed in a miniskirt, long blonde hair, dangley earrings, high heels and panty hose – the works. This person usually saw my partner so I didn't know this patient's history. Luckily for me, the nurse clued me in – the patient was a cross-dressing man. He/she came in because of a cough, so after I examined his ears and throat, I said, "Bill, would you please remove your bra so I can listen to your chest?"

When I was interning at a county hospital in a Western state, mothers could request suggestions for naming their new babies. Our beloved hospital administrator, C. Otis Whitecotten has a number of children named after him in the area.

• • •

A young boy visited my partner after a nose injury. The doctor suggested to his mother he get a x-ray of his nose to check for a broken nose. The mother demurred. Then the doctor added, "You don't want a nose that looks like Dr. Briggs', do you?" With this, she promptly went to the x-ray department.

• • •

Not everyone can do this, but a doctor can. One of our two sons seemed to miss the toilet regularly. We just weren't sure which one. I gave one a methylene pill that turns the urine blue. Sherlock Holmes wasn't needed to nail the culprit.

While skiing in Aspen some years ago, I fell and broke my nose. When I got back to the house I took the smooth handle of a fork and inserted it into my nose to push the bones back into place. After that, everyone was worried that they were using "that" fork, even though it had been run through the dishwasher.

As a rather baby-faced intern, I arrived at the expectant mother's side prior to delivering her baby. She said, "Here I am in all this misery, and they send me a boy."

A medical school professor was teaching a section on venereal disease. He stated, "Some people will put their manhood where I wouldn't put my walking stick."

• • •

A worried mother brought in her little boy who had swallowed something he wasn't supposed to. The radiologist asked the family after x-raying the child if there was something with a chain missing. Yes, there was. The doctor successfully delivered the Our Father and two Hail Mary beads from a rosary.

• • •

A 12-year-old was asked by the doctor to get up on the end of the examining table. When the doctor turned around, the boy was standing on the end of the examining table, with his head bent to avoid hitting his head on the ceiling.

When the man was in the operating room, the surgeon lifted the sheet to find the patient had written across each toe, "F-R-O-N-T."

In medical school, when we study a new disease, it usually crosses our mind that perhaps we have one of these diseases. One of our fellow students carried this to the extreme. He felt sure that he had just about every disease we studied. In fact, he was so sure he had to see one of the professors to be sure that he didn't have TB, malaria, yaws, etc., etc.

• • •

Finesse is a trait learned by a doctor. As a new physician, I was attending my ten-year class reunion. I commented to a woman from my class, "When are you expecting?" And her glared reply was, "I had it five months ago."

• • •

When my son was 8-year-old, we were discussing delivering babies. He said, "Dad, when you take a baby, do you close your eyes?"

During a surgery lecture, I asked the professor why, if gall stones are small, they don't fall out of the gallbladder – that is, they aren't always big. The professor replied, "You're going to go a long ways, but not in surgery."

• • •

A woman was diagnosed with fibroids, benign tumors in the uterus. She laughingly told the doctor she misunderstood and told her husband she had "fireballs in her uterus."

• • •

An elderly female patient said to her gynecologist while he was examining her, "Young man, does your mother know what you do for a living?"

The burglar alarm went off at the clinic and I was called. I arrived at the clinic to find it surrounded by police with drawn guns. I started out of my car only to be stopped by a sergeant asking me to go back across the parking lot.

I assumed they were keeping me back for my safety. However, I learned later from a nurse who monitors police radio calls that this conversation took place: "Would you check the license number on a white Thunderbird License No. LM 487." Then the answer came back telling him that the car belonged to the doctor who alleges he's Dr. Briggs. Then the officer said, "Jeez, I haven't seen him in ten years; I bet he's put on 50 pounds."

• • •

Doctors get involved in all kinds of logistical predicaments. During the days when doctors made house calls, Dr. James thought he'd seen it all. A rather heavy-set woman had slid off the toilet seat and wedged herself between the wall and the toilet. After attempting to get out by herself, she had to call her boyfriend. He, too, couldn't help extract her. When the doctor arrived, someone had the bright idea to apply cooking lard between the wall and the women and the toilet bowl. With everyone pulling, the compressed woman was delivered to safety.

After discovering there was too much accounts receivable and not enough money coming in, a small town doctor decided it was time to be more direct with his patients. He trained his beautiful parrot, a tropical macaw bird, to say, "Get the cash, get the cash!"

I always wondered about the vigilance and responsibility of parents whose children swallowed poisons – until it happened to me twice in two weeks. The first time happened a few days after I graduated from medical school. Our two-and-a-half-year-old son was hyperactive. My mother-in-law knew this and saw to it that her house was "safe" when we came by, hiding mouse pellets high on a shelf in the closet. I was to help my father-in-law pour a cement car port. When I was ankle-deep in cement, my mother-in-law burst out of the door to announce our son was on the closet floor munching on the mouse pellets containing strychnine. My wife rushed him to a nearby clinic for treatment.

• • •

Two weeks later, I had arrived at my internship destination in Oakland, California. I was washing our car in the driveway when I looked up to see this same son squatting in the grass lifting a small green bottle to his mouth. I inspected the bottle and noted it was Terro ant poison containing arsenic. It had been left there by the apartment caretaker. I rushed our son to the emergency room of my new hospital. A plastic naso-gastric tube/stomach tube was placed in his stomach and ants could be seen coming out through the clear plastic.

Three expecting women were in two different hospitals. The doctor tried his best to scurry from one room to the next to the other hospital to deliver all the babies. He managed to miss all three!

• • •

The speaker said at the medical convention that he opened his Gideon Bible and noticed some quotations. One said, "If you are sad, read John 1:3; if you are lonely, read Corinthians 4:25." Penciled in below, "If you are still lonely, call Barbie, 476-3578."

• • •

This same doctor said, "Behind every successful man is an amazed mother-in-law."

A married patient went to Mexico to study Spanish. While there, she became involved with a Mexican man and became pregnant. Shocked and in a desperate hope of subterfuge, she rushed home to have intercourse with her husband.

It was an exercise in futility because when her baby was finally delivered, her secret was out. As the baby's head showed, it might as well have worn a sombrero hat it was so obviously Mexican. The doctor was glad to miss her "explanation" to her shocked husband.

The phone rang in the clinic during the early evening hours. A patient well-known to me but not the staff, told the receptionist that a bus load was on its way to the clinic with about 20 people suffering from nausea, vomiting and diarrhea! He suspected it was food poisoning from a fund-raising dinner to buy a new trombone for the church choir.

The staff was frantic wondering how to handle all these patients. When I heard the story and the name of the perpetrator, I knew it was a hoax.

• • •

A friend bought a doctor an inexpensive Rolex look-alike watch as a gift which he presented at lunch. The friend thought it would be fun to tell the doctor the watch could talk. This seemed to the friend that it could possibly work because the doctor was getting hard of hearing.

The friend said, "Did you hear that?"

The doctor said, "Hear what?"

The friend said, "Your watch, it just said, 'it's one o'clock."

The doctor said, "It's an inexpensive watch, it wouldn't talk.

IT'S ONE O'CLOCK

The friend then gives the other guys they lunched with a poke under the table, and then they all agreed they had heard the watch talk.

He later called my wife to clue her in.

Later that evening, the doctor and his wife and another couple were driving to a friend's house for dinner. The wife said, "Did you hear that?"

The doctor said, "Hear what?"

The wife said, "Your watch said it was seven o'clock." And the other couple said they had heard it too.

The doctor now was starting to believe the talking watch was real, maybe.

At the dinner table, the wife of the host couple said, "Doc, your watch just said it is 7:30."

About 8 p.m., the doctor removed his watch and put it up to his ear because they all claimed they could hear the watch say "8:00." The doctor shrugged and became more of a believer as he said, "It must be out of my hearing range."

At 8 the next morning, the staff was assembled for our regular staff meeting. We were waiting for the remainder of the staff to come when I remembered my talking watch. I said, "Hey, you've got to hear this." and I held the watch out.

Of course, nothing happened and they all looked at me as if to say, "the old doc's lost it."

That wasn't the end. The doctor DID buy a watch that could talk. He lunched with the same four men, including the friend who bought him the first watch. At a quarter to the hour, the watch not only talked, a rooster crowed. When the doctor let his friends listen to his crowing watch . . . they did it to him again. "We didn't hear anything," they said in unison.

• • •

My wife's bridge group was told this watch story. Everyone laughed heartily, except for one elderly lady. They asked, "What's wrong, Millie?" The dear soul replied, "I don't think it's very funny, your making fun of my doctor!" They reassured her that I had laughed as hard as any of them.

A close friend of mine came to see me because of a questionable lump on his prostate. I sent my friend, an airline pilot, to see a urologist. This doctor had a sense of humor much like my pilot friend. With the biopsy needle in place, the doctor jabbed for a specimen and said, "This is for those late departures" and at the second jab, he said, "and this is for those rough landings."

• • •

I had a patient who worked as a prostitute in Montana. The authorities did weekly checks to be sure they were clear of venereal disease. My patient took a "working holiday" to Oklahoma City and was staying at a hotel. While there, she caught syphilis. I asked her how many tricks she turned a night. She replied, "About eight – I get tired, you know."

• • •

When my wife and I are out socially, many friends ask me medical questions. My wife has gotten so she gives the answers to many of the questions before I have time to reply.

A friend of mine who is about 5'6" has nine children. A doctor, who was 6'5" moved next door. My friends two little boys rushed home and said, "Dad, dad, a giant has moved in next door!"

I was standing against the blank wall at the foot of the bed. The patient was an alcoholic who was hallucinating. He asked me to move so he could see the TV.

• • •

Sago palm extract is used in New Guinea to make Sago palm pancakes. We visited the natives there and watched the process. A 100-foot tree was selected, chopped down, and cut up into six-foot sections. These in turn were split and the center was pulpified by pounding. Then followed running water down the center, the extract collected and the paste was fried on a grill to make the pancake. They looked and tasted like what I would imagine plaster of Paris would taste like.

This experience took on greater consequences later on with one of my patients who had been stationed in Guam. He presented me with a letter from the Veteran's Administration that stated if he had any symptoms of Parkinson's Disease, to see their physician because perhaps these symptoms may be associated with eating Sago palm pancakes.

I interned in Oakland, California. We took care of a large nursing home with rows of beds. At night the patients looked the same as they lay on their backs, and mouths open. Each bed had tennis net strung over it like a mosquito net to restrain them if they tried to get out of bed and also to prevent injury.

As the attending doctor, we would be called out at night to pronounce a death. Since all nursing home residents looked the same asleep, we'd check the ones that weren't snoring or we couldn't feel any air coming out of their lungs. If we were still puzzled, we'd ask the nurses who they suspected had died.

• • •

Newly-hired staff at our clinic had to pass my "lice" hurdle. Under a microscope a head, body or pubic louse looks much like a crab with pincers and claws. When alive and magnified, the claws are very crab-like. I've had many of the new personnel jump back with alarm as this "crab" flexed his claws and pincers.

On our trip to New Guinea, my friend and I were "honored" to wear the ceremonial wig and warrior wig of the chief. After we'd worn these wigs, we noticed the chief had significant head lice. Luckily, neither of us caught any hitchhikers.

• • •

I served as a flight surgeon in the U.S. Air Force. One of my duties was to standby when Russian President Nikita Khrushchev's airliner landed at Andrews Air Base, Washington, D.C. In case of any medical emergencies, I was to be prepared.

One of the stewardesses on board this huge Russian "Bear" aircraft fell down a flight of stairs inside the plane. I was one of four Americans to go on board. When I examined her leg, I noted she had more hair on hers than I had on mine!

• • •

A colleague was giving a sex education lecture. One of the students asked, "Can you get VD off a toilet seat."

"Yes," the doctor replied, "but it is a very uncomfortable position."

A North Dakota colleague tells about a very bad day for one of his patients:

The man was sawing and accidently cut his thumb. He grabbed a rag (which happened to be doused in turpentine), and when he wrapped it around thumb, it caused him to scream. He then sat down on a nylon webbed lawn chair and lit a cigarette. This caused the turpentine to catch fire around his hand. To get up quickly, he put his hand on the webbed chair and it caught fire. He ran up to the farm house hollering for his wife to help. She opened the door to his screams and he ran into the edge of the door and fractured his nose.

An elderly woman continued to see her doctor who was also in his early '80s. Her daughter suggested her mother should see a younger physician. The daughter encouraged the mother to tell the doctor she was changing physicians on her next visit.

The daughter asked, "What did he say," and mother said, "I don't know, as I was reading my lists of concerns, he fell asleep."

As we get older, we get lots of aches and pains. I tell my older patients, "I'd rather have you wear out than rust out."

• • •

I gave my friend's wife some bulk producing fiber pills. She thought if one was good, six would be six times as good. She described her elimination as "passing bales of hay."

• • •

A couple, friends of ours, wanted to deliver their baby at home. I thought I'd talked her out of it after I explained the risk of bleeding, and lack of resuscitation equipment if the baby need it. But the mother-to-be waited too long and we had a home delivery. The delivery went well, using the dining room table, two high chairs reversed for stirrups. Results: healthy baby and happy mother.

My wife assisted me and she'd never witnessed a delivery before. That night she had nightmares in technicolor. I often wonder what a window peeper would think if he saw this scene.

The pathologist at the hospital prepared three lung specimens in plastic bags for me to show to patients. I used the lung specimens to try to encourage his most-determined smokers to quit.

One specimen had been affected by cancer of the lung, one by emphysema, however, one was normal, for comparison. After a smoker patient got a good look at the lungs, he looked again at the nondiseased lung, and said, "If he's so normal, what's he doing in the bag?"

For Men Only ...

A woman was having her annual pelvic exam, and her doctor was a long-time friend.

She appeared for the exam, and for a joke, appeared in her Fredericks of Hollywood panties that didn't require removal for a pelvic exam.

...

In the orthopedic ward where I interned, I noticed there was a man with a long leg cast in overhead traction. A fly swatter was hanging off the traction frame. "What's that for?" I asked.

"When the maggots hatch and the flies come out, I swat them!" the man said. Apparently he had been drunk and was hit by a car. It wasn't until the next day when he was found. He had a compound fracture that caused a severe infection. The infection was infested with maggots. During a cast change, maggots could be seen crawling in the wound.

Our receptionist greeted an elderly man who didn't hear well. "How are you?"

"What did you say," he asked her.

She raised her voice and said, "Hi, Mr. Brown, How Are You?"

"I got worms, you want to see them," he asked, and proceeded to unwrap his wound.

The receptionist quickly ushered him to an examining room. The man had burned himself and to sterilize the wound, put bleach on it, causing a lot of dead tissue, a perfect breeding ground for his maggots.

• • •

People put strange things into their body openings – ears, nose, vagina, and rectum. One colleague was brought to tears by having to peel an onion to remove it from a rectum.

Strange things happen to penises, too. A young man came in with a rather raw end of his penis. It was caused by having it dangle in some water in the toilet bowl that had some strong cleaning solution in it.

• • •

A tattoo on the lower abdomen of a female patient: Sailors' entrance in the rear.

• • •

When in medical school in the '50s, we had several Spanish American war veterans as patients. Those who had large prostrates, we said "came dribbling in to Iowa City (Iowa) to have their rifle bores cleaned out."

• • •

My partner approached me one day with his sly grin that usually provokes laughter before he's even told me his latest encounter. He said his patient declared she had a yeast infection, but she'd "licked it herself." He paused and said, "Tom, I didn't say a word."

Would You Believe ...?

During an operation for an abdominal abscess, a toothpick was pulled out of the abscess. The patient reported he had a pig-in-the-blanket sausage and pancake for breakfast. He also had eaten the toothpick used to hold it all together. This troublesome toothpick perforated the bowel causing the abdominal abscess.

• • •

Having spent time with Mother Theresa in India, I knew that lepers frequently have anesthesia of their arms and legs. When sleeping in the streets, they get bitten by rats without knowing it. They come in with sores on their arms and legs from the bites.

• • •

A middle-aged woman entered our drug treatment center. The relatives who accompanied her carried shopping bags and shoe boxes filled with pills and bags of marijuana. This combination weighted about 25 pounds. She took an estimated 60 different pills a day. We figured she didn't have any room for food and would just pour a little gravy over her pills and would have a meal!

As a medical consultant to a womens' alcohol unit, I was called in to see a woman in severe DTs. We were unable to keep a nightgown on her as she would repeatedly take it off and tear it up into shreds. When she finally came around three or four days later, we asked her what she was hallucinating. She said she would see Cossack dancers with their flashing knives, and as they wheeled around, they would lop off a hand or an arm or leg, which would cause spurting of blood. She was tearing up her nightgown to make tourniquets to stop the bleeding

• • •

Some of my patients in alcoholic treatment drink prodigious quantities of alcohol. I've had three or four patients that have drunk two cases of beer per day. One would think the patient might drown before they'd get drunk! And I'm sure they would have to stay close to the restroom.

I had a young man who was able to drink four quarts of whiskey daily. Yet, I had another young woman who was an alcoholic on three beers a day. On one beer she was high, two she was drunk, and three she was out of her mind. At age 21, she had ten DWIs (driving while intoxicated) violations.

When I was in the military, it was during the time Gary Powers was shot down over Russia in his U2 surveillance airplane. Another flyer came in claiming that he was a U2 pilot too. We all scoffed at him and notified higher authorities. We later learned that he really was a U2 pilot and was going psychotic. He was immediately interviewed by the CIA.

• • •

Another of my duties as a flight surgeon was to take care of the pilots of F106 air defense squadron. I was able to fly with the commander at twice the speed of sound.

The commander had a unique way of treating his sinus infections. There is a technique in medicine called Proetz displacement in which alternating negative and positive pressure allows a decongestant into the nose to displace the mucus and open and drain the sinus passages. The commander would take his F106 straight up to 40,000 feet. The air pressure would expand with altitude and blow the mucus out of his sinuses. Then he would temporarily remove his oxygen mask and inhale a decongestant spray into his nose. Following this he would rapidly descend and drive the decongestant into his sinuses. After he landed, he could breathe much easier!

A Funny Thing Happened at the Doctor's Office
Order Form

Need another copy for a friend or for the office? You can order directly from:

Beaver's Pond Press

5125 Danen's Drive   Edina, MN 55439-1465
Phone: (612) 829-8818
Fax: (612) 944-4065
e-mail: adamsppo@aol.com

Number of Copies	___ x	$6.95 ___
Shipping – One Book		$1.95 ___
Shipping – Additional Copies ___ x		$1.00 ___

TOTAL ORDER ___

Payment enclosed: ❑ Check   ❑ Money Order

SHIPPING ADDRESS

Name (please print) _____

Address _____

City _____ *State* _____ *Zip* _____

Telephone (___) _____